Popular Performer

Christmas Just for You

Arranged by DENNIS ALEXANDER

10 Popular Songs of the Season

When I was in college, I played in a private club every weekend for several years. Each Christmas season, I wished that I had a collection of popular Christmas songs arranged in a variety of styles to share with my audiences, friends, and family.

With that wish in mind, I arranged my personal favorites for *Christmas Just for You*. I hope that you will have as much fun playing them as I had in writing the arrangements! Included are lush, romantic harmonies in "Blue Christmas" and "Home for the Holidays." Jazzy versions of "Santa Baby," "Let There Be Peace on Earth," and "Mistletoe and Holly" will bring a smile to your face. Sounds from the Hawaiian islands prevail in "Mele Kalikimaka." And if you enjoy Jim Brickman's song "The Gift" as much as I do, you will discover a new twist to this audience favorite!

Merry Christmas to you and yours! May your holiday season be blessed with love, good music, and much happiness.

Dennis Alexander

CONTENTS

Blue Christmas 2

Feliz Navidad 38

The Gift 22

(There's No Place Like) Home for the Holidays 30

Let There Be Peace on Earth. 14

Mary, Did You Know? 6

Mele Kalikimaka 26

Mistletoe and Holly. 10

Rockin' Around the Christmas Tree 34

Santa Baby 18

Produced by
Alfred Music
P.O. Box 10003
Van Nuys, CA 91410-0003
alfred.com

D1275476

Produced in USA.

ISBN-10: 0-7390-8757-6
ISBN-13: 978-0-7390-8757-2

Cover art
Vintage Christmas Decorations: © shutterstock / Subbotina Anna

Blue Christmas

Words and Music by
Bill Hayes and Jay Johnson
Arr. Dennis Alexander

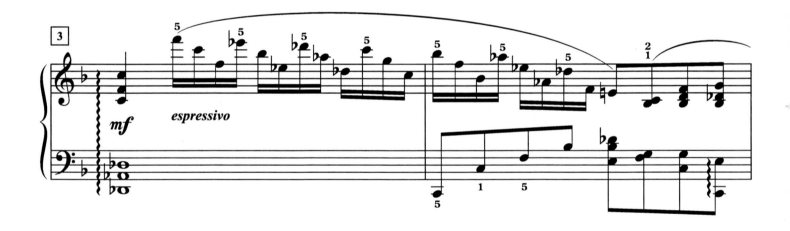

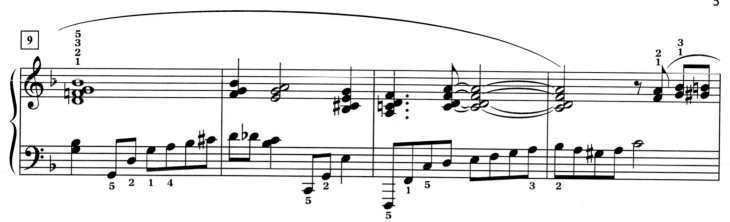

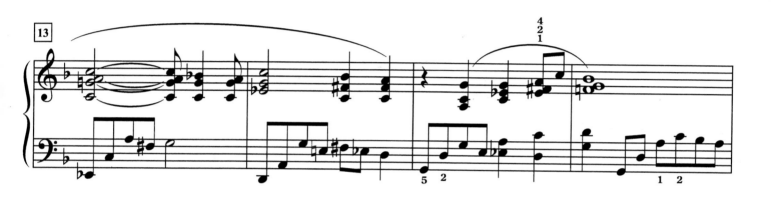

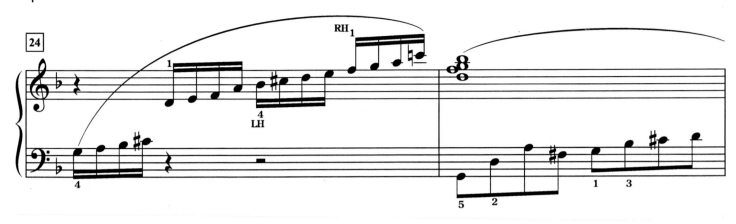

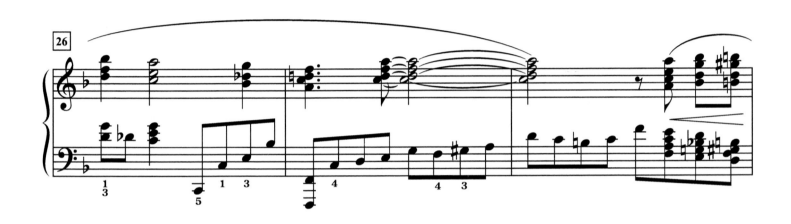

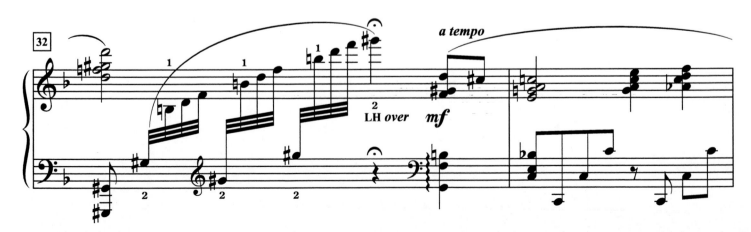

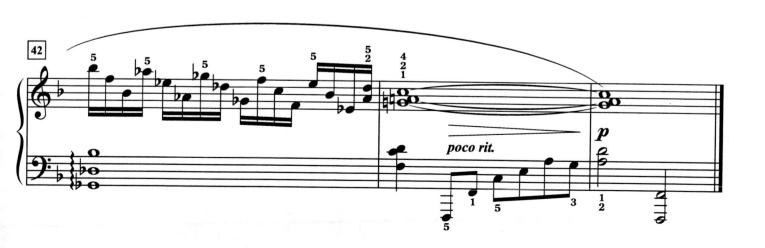

Mary, Did You Know?

Words and Music by
Mark Lowry and Buddy Greene
Arr. Dennis Alexander

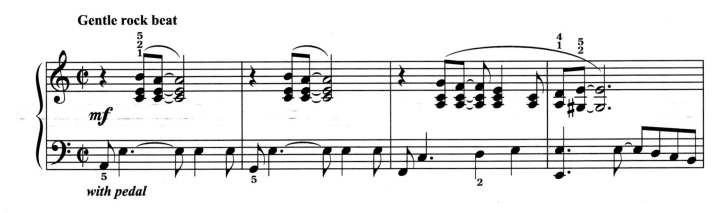

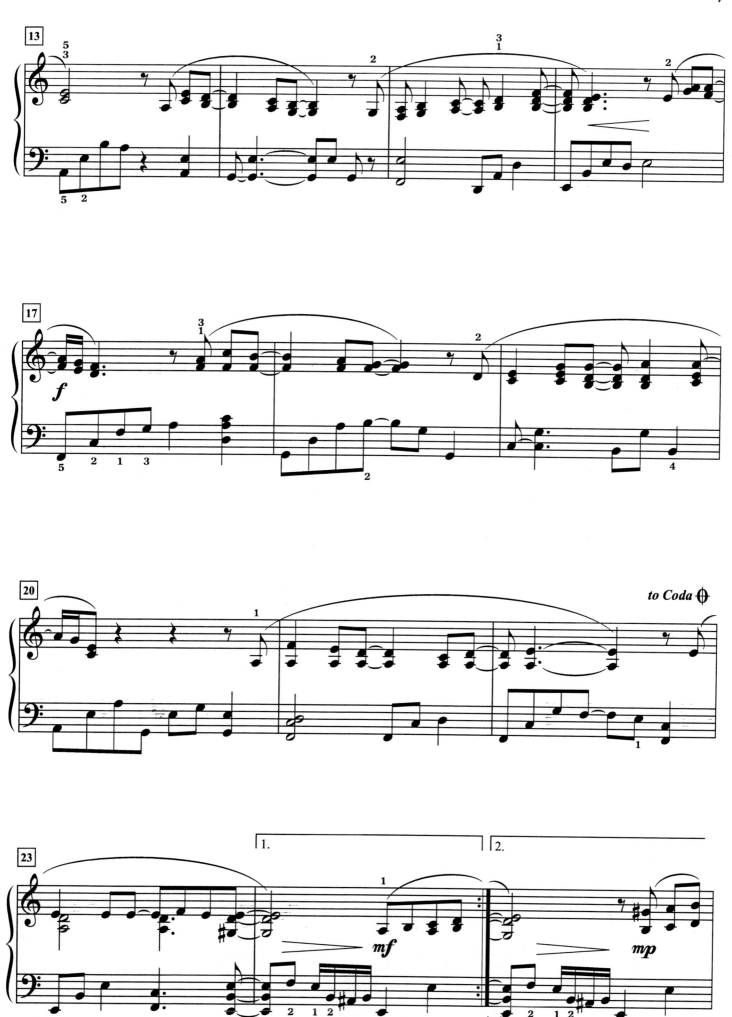

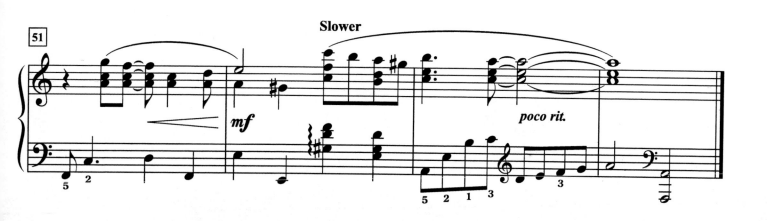

MISTLETOE AND HOLLY

Words and Music by
Frank Sinatra, Dok Stanford and Henry Sanicola
Arr. Dennis Alexander

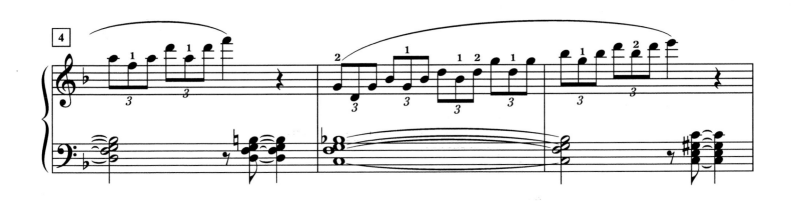

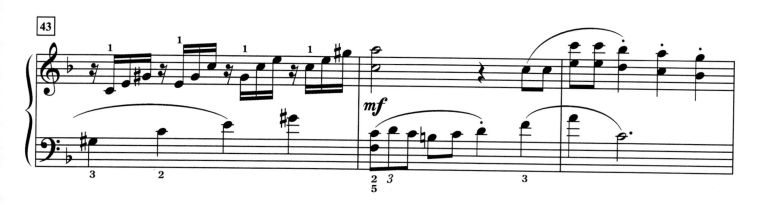

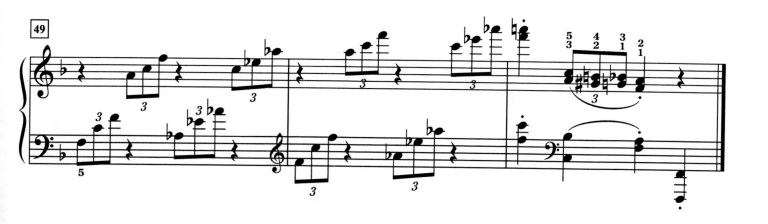

Let There Be Peace On Earth

Words and Music by
Sy Miller and Jill Jackson
Arr. Dennis Alexander

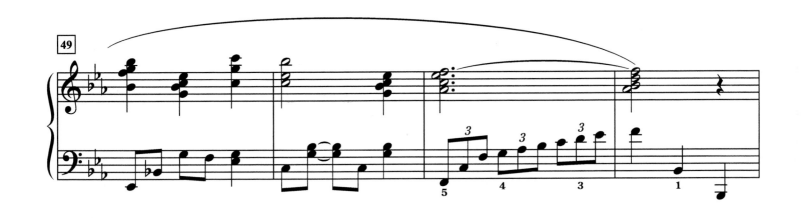

Santa Baby

Words and Music by
Joan Javits, Philip Springer and Tony Springer
Arr. Dennis Alexander

Relaxed, and freely

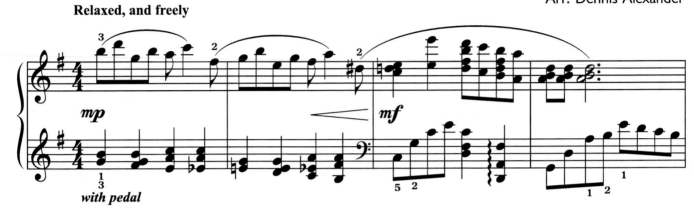

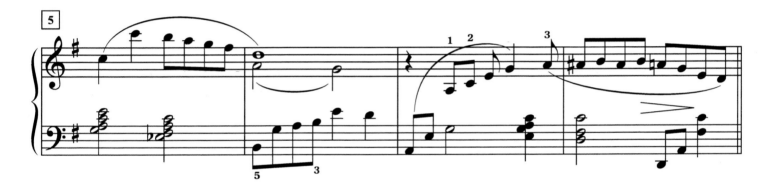

Bright, swing tempo

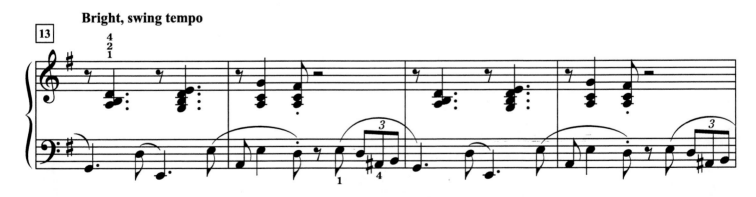

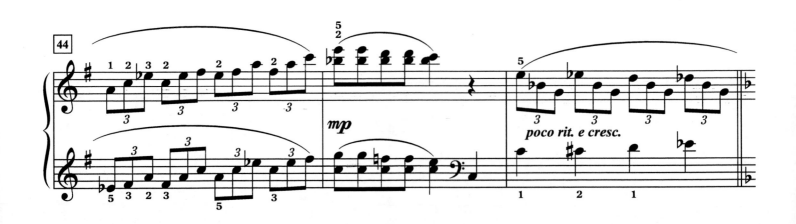

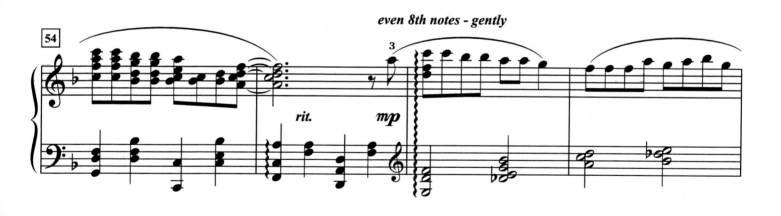

THE GIFT

Words and Music by
Jim Brickman and Tom Douglas
Arr. Dennis Alexander

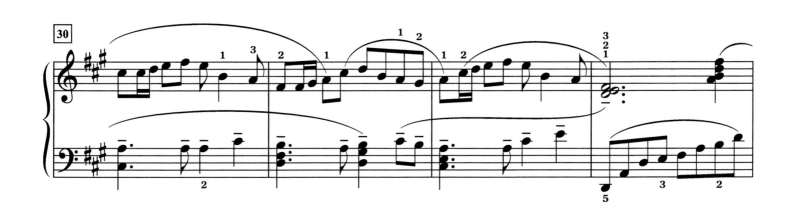

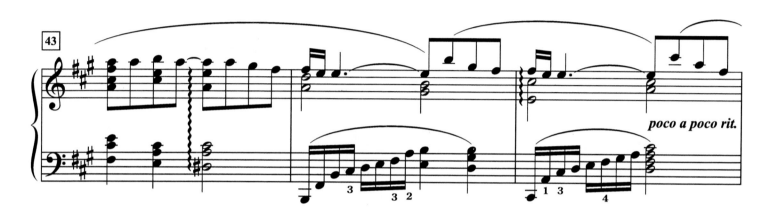

Mele Kalikimaka

Words and Music by R. Alex Anderson
Arr. Dennis Alexander

(There's No Place Like) Home For The Holidays

Words by Al Stillman
Music by Robert Allen
Arr. Dennis Alexander

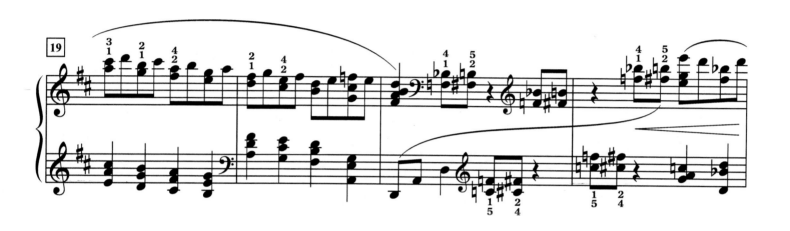

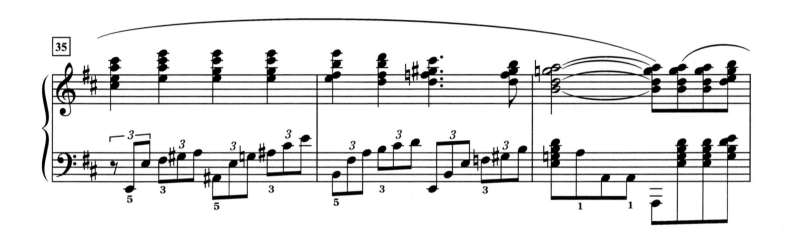

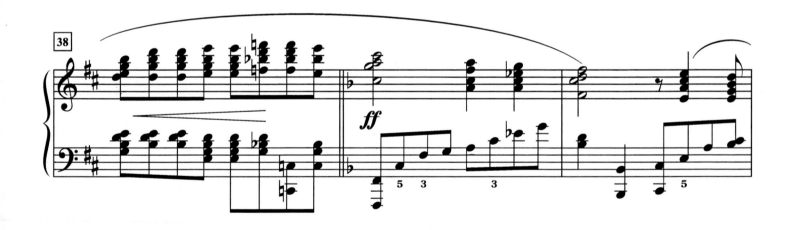

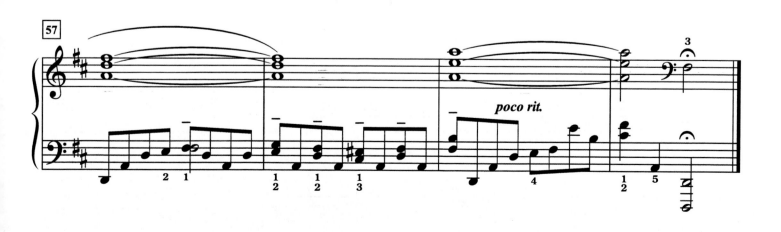

Rockin' Around the Christmas Tree

Words and Music by Johnny Marks
Arr. Dennis Alexander

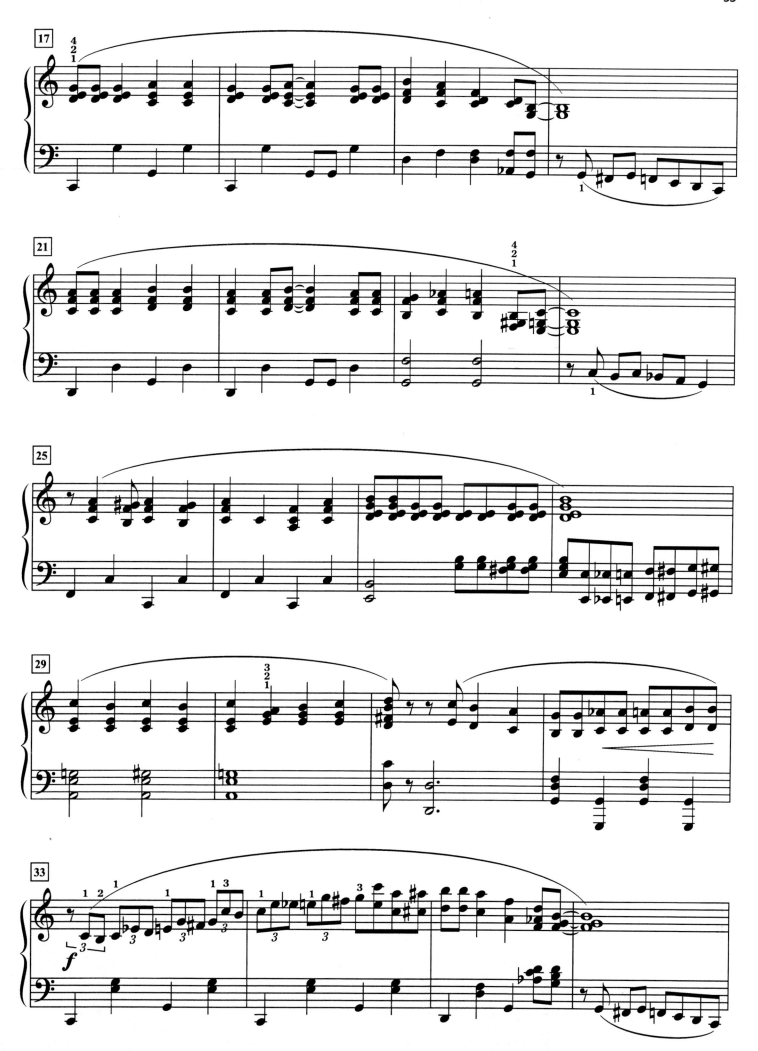

FELIZ NAVIDAD

Words and Music by José Feliciano
Arr. Dennis Alexander

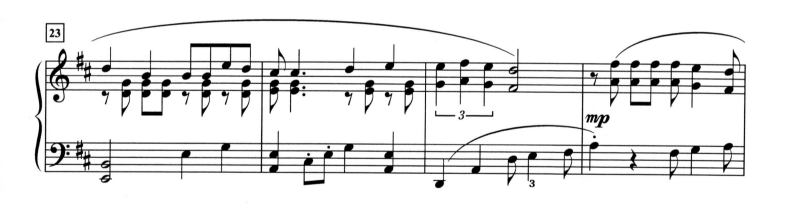

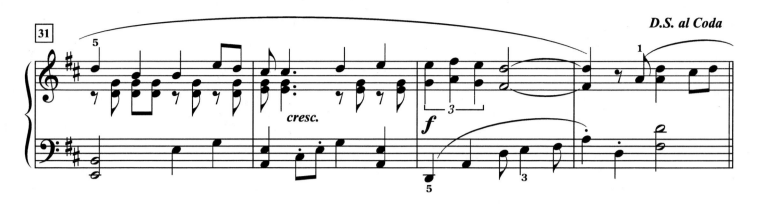

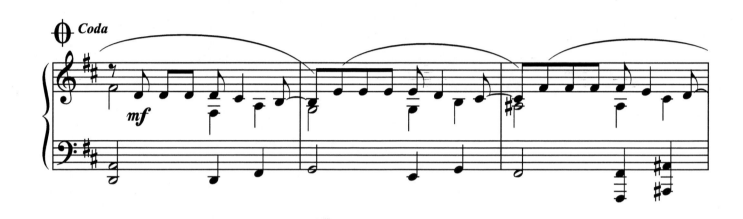

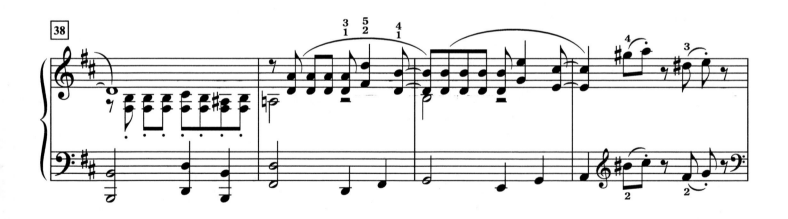